The Four Ethics

Navigating Life Authentically

Marilyn Cornelius

DEDICATION

For Sashi and Noji.

Table of Contents

ACKNOWLEDGMENTS

My gratitude extends to Margaret (Ma) for her editing powers and unconditional love, and to Nathaniel (Daddy) for being unconditionally supportive and for reading and providing feedback on the outline of this book. Many thanks to Emily for receiving and reading the proof.

Preface

How This Book Came to Be

After five years of channeling books, last night I went to bed and soon thereafter had to get up to make a note in my phone about an idea that descended into my mind gently, as all intuitive ideas do. The idea was about four basic foundations for a mindful and love-filled life. That idea forms the basis of this book.

I was in progress with two other books, one in Alchemus Prime's leadership series and the other a poetry collaboration that is being published through my company. This book came unannounced. I woke up this morning and outlined the book. Then I sat at my desk and drafted it within a couple of hours. This is how books come to me and through me – swiftly.

The Four Ethics is about a thread that we can see clearly if we look at reality: harm. We are harming each other through relationships, politics, climate change, and in many other ways. To avoid harm, we must first stop harming ourselves. We often damage ourselves through our self-doubt and negative self-talk. The root of this is abuse and trauma encountered early in life.

We must go within to remove trauma and love the self. This self-love forms the foundation of everything, as I have elaborated on in *The Path to Romantic Success: What You Won't Learn in School or at Home about Finding True Love,* and in my video show on social media, Mornings with Marilyn. My book on trauma: *From Abused to Empowered: Recognizing and Releasing Behavior Patterns that come from Trauma*, provides real case studies that help us get to the root of our harmful behavior patterns and heal.

The Four Ethics

An ethic is a set of moral principles. This book, as is true for many of my other books, is about behavior. How we conduct ourselves is the strongest indicator of who we are. Ethics guide us and our behavior defines us. It is incumbent upon each of us to make sure that it is our authenticity, not our trauma, that is steering our behavior each day of our lives.

The Four Ethics is a compass for navigating life. In these interconnected chapters, I aim to clearly and succinctly present four core ideas to help us live more fulfilling lives. Each chapter has short sub-sections that explain what each ethic means, how to practice it, exceptions to be aware of, and how to set boundaries based on the ethic.

Allow the content of this book to become assimilated into your mind and translated through your communication, behavior, and self-care. Begin to notice the difference you feel once you put these guidelines into motion.

My love and blessings are with you, all the way, and always.

Marilyn Cornelius
October 6, 2020
Suva
Fiji

Marilyn Cornelius

1

The Ethic of Avoiding Harm

Don't intentionally harm anyone

"If you can, help others; if you cannot do that, at least do not harm them."

— Dalai Lama XIV

Ensure Positive Actions Toward Self and Everyone Else

It is important to think of ourselves as conduits of energy. We want to send out positive energy, signals, thoughts, words, and especially actions into the world. We may be motivated to do this because of how we think about karma: what goes around comes around. However, it's important to be a positive force in the world because *it's the right thing to do*. This also relates to the Ethic of Integrity (Chapter 3), as we will see.

If we are able to cultivate positivity within, we can share it outwardly. So, the work is always inner work. Uprooting all forms of negativity, including self-judgment, low self-esteem, negative self-talk, and the three self no-nos: self-doubt, self-loathing, and self-sabotage,[1] are crucial to becoming a genuine source of positivity.

If Your Trauma Patterns are Creating Harm, Get Help to Change Your Behavior and Heal

Typically, at the root of negativity within us, lies abuse and trauma. Many, if not all of us, have been abused in some way when we were younger. This can range from sexual, physical, emotional or psychological, to verbal abuse, which leads to lingering traumatic effects.

Sometimes, we are too young to remember being abused, or our minds block it out because it was too painful. However, the body always remembers the affects of abuse, and there are often lasting effects in the subconscious mind. These can be observed through chronic anxiety, fear, depression, paranoia,

---

[1] See *The Path to Romantic Success: What You Won't Learn in School or at Home about Finding True Love* for more on the three self no-nos.

anger bursts, or apathy.

Childhood trauma controls our behavior patterns as adults. These behavior patterns include being controlling and manipulative, lying, being narcissistic, or playing the victim. Trauma can infiltrate every aspect of our lives, from relationships to career paths. To feel the truth of this, think about the most difficult people in your life. Do they exhibit these tendencies? Chances are they were abused and are now displaying these harmful coping mechanisms.

The starting point is to become aware that we are in a trauma pattern and creating or sustaining harm. It involves admitting to ourselves that we are part of the problem, whether as perpetrators, victims, or both. Often, we become identified with our traumatized self, mistaking it for our true self. To break free of this, it is crucial to have an outside perspective, because friends and family often become codependent with us. That is, our patterns and their patterns find harmful yet comfortable ways to interact and co-exist.

To be shown that our lives are made up of trauma patterns can be very disheartening. It requires tremendous courage and humility, the release of any arrogance, and honesty with the self, to begin the journey of healing our trauma.

To release yourself from trauma, it is important to secure the help of a skilled coach or therapist who is focused on applying proven tools and changing behavior. Transformative change is possible with the help of a coach and these three qualities within you: readiness to change, willingness to do the hard work, and commitment to the self, as evidenced by investment in the process.[2] When these three qualities are present, a person can create a remarkable change within, which then emanates as improved relationships, more positive outlooks on life, and optimal career changes.[3]

Exceptions

There are some instances in life when you cannot avoid harm. You may have to intentionally harm someone. For instance, when you are defending life. It could be a life-threatening situation in which you are attacked, and you might have to resort to restraining your attacker or physically harming them in self-defense.

---

[2] Based on observations of over 55 clients in our Lasting Transformation (coaching) program.

[3] Based on the transformative changes seen in clients who go through our Lasting Transformation and Career Manifestation Programs.

Perhaps you need to protect the life of someone who is vulnerable, such as a child or animal who is being abused. In such cases, we may need to inflict harm to avoid injury or worse to the victim of the attack.

Life is never black and white, which is what makes ethics an intriguing and lifelong inquiry. In general, this rule of thumb will serve us well in life: avoid harming anyone intentionally, except to protect and save a life.

Boundaries

If we willingly or subconsciously allow ourselves to be harmed by others, we will continue to prevent our growth as professional, intellectual, emotional, and spiritual beings. We should set boundaries based on avoiding harm whenever we can; this helps us respect ourselves and live better lives, with less negative energy.

Harm can manifest in many other ways, not just as a physical attack. For example, if we are in an abusive work situation, where our supervisor constantly berates us, it is important to speak up and ask to be treated with compassion (Chapter 4). If we do not, then we have no self-respect or self-love (Chapter 2), and we are not setting effective boundaries to help us feel safe to work and flourish.

When we carry the trauma of past abuse, it can be difficult to set good boundaries, because our self-worth is tainted by the trauma we feel within. It is important to go into that trauma and heal it. If we do not, we remain trapped by these trauma patterns, and we will continue to set weak boundaries or not have boundaries at all.

Reflection:
1. What harmful situations do you find yourself in right now?
   a. How might you set better boundaries to protect yourself in these situations?
2. What exceptions, if any, are you making right now, with regard to harm, and why?
3. What would be the ideal resolution to each of the situations you described?
   a. How might you achieve these solutions?

The Four Ethics

2

The Ethic of Self-Love

*Love yourself first so you can learn to love and be
loved by others*

*"How you love yourself is
how you teach others
to love you."*

— Rupi Kaur

Become Your Own Best Friend

Too often, we are our own biggest critics. We have that punishing voice that we inflict on ourselves whenever we make a mistake. Perhaps it comes from a parent or a teacher, and we can notice the root of this habit if we observe and reflect carefully. We must remove this tendency if we are to be successful (and by that I mean happy) beings.

It is important to treat yourself as you would an innocent child, a best friend, or an esteemed elder: with patience, affection and kindness. Imagine the people you love the most, and would do anything for. Now add yourself to the top of that list. It isn't easy because hardly anyone teaches us self-love, but this is the foundation of all our relationships – personal and professional.

Take the Time to Get to Know Yourself – Your True Self

One of the most effective ways to develop the habit of self-love is to be alone. Spending quality time with ourselves allows us to learn more about what makes us feel happy, comfortable, and accepted by ourselves. This last point is critical, because too often we want to be liked by others and feel disappointed when we are not. It is far more important to like ourselves, so we can be free of others' opinions.

Some important ways to spend time with ourselves is to explore our interests. Taking classes, going to gatherings, and exploring topics to see what we might enjoy is an essential step in understanding and developing ourselves. This allows us to discover and support who we really are, which is a first step in offering our true selves to any other relationship.[4]

Develop Your Strengths

As we begin to learn about our likes and dislikes, we will also discover what we are really good at. Perhaps it's a skill or a talent that was lying untapped before. With this new information, we can find ways to develop those strengths. This is one reason many of us stay stuck in careers we hate: we haven't taken the time to explore what we love and what we are good at, and we don't have the confidence to go after what we truly want to actualize at the soul level.

Once we emerge from the trap of mediocre jobs and embrace our true calling, we shift our careers in magnificent ways. Our forthcoming book, *Career Manifestation: What it Takes to be Who You Truly Are in a World that Wants You to be Someone Else*, written by Dr. Margaret Cornelius, shares the story of how a lifetime can be spent to refine our true calling, navigating life's priorities along the way. Education, marriage, family, and career challenges can sometimes all hit us at once, but with passion, partnership and perseverance, we can achieve our dreams.

---

[4] For more on how to achieve self-love, see *The Path to Romantic Success: What You Won't Learn in School or at Home about Finding True Love.*

Exceptions

We may think we need to neglect the self to care for our child or elder, but the truth is that if we are impaired, the quality of the care we give to others will be diminished. It is imperative that we prioritize self-love as a foundation in our lives, so we can give of our best selves.

There may be extreme situations where you must choose between spending time alone because you need to recharge, or spending time with a suicidal loved one, for instance. This is a tricky situation because you may feel obligated to spend time with your loved one to prevent them from harming themselves.

If we do choose them over ourselves, it is important to make time for ourselves later and bring ourselves back to full strength, and to alert others of our loved one's mental state so more help could be garnered for their well being. We must also consider the quality of our presence; if we are impaired and exhausted, we may share that vibration with our loved one, which could further lower their mood.

Boundaries

As you learn to love yourself and begin to prioritize yourself, those who were accustomed to your old, traumatized self may not like it. They may now resent you because you have changed. Set boundaries that allow those who do not like your true self to fall away and make room for real relationships. The sad truth is that many people position themselves around us to derive benefits from us; when we become more authentic, they are unable to continue as they desire. Do not accept blame for becoming a better person; instead let them go (Chapter 3) with compassion (Chapter 4).

It can be a lonely time and it hurts to lose people you thought were your real friends and family. However, it helps to shift your focus. Notice who supports you and prioritizes you as you are evolving, and be sure to make time for these gems. They are the ones who deserve your time and energy, because they are not trying to use you for some outcome they want. They are genuine and will be with you all the way. This is your tribe.[5]

---

[5] For more on how to navigate what can be a lonely and challenging period, see *The Path to Romantic Success: What You Won't Learn in School or at Home about Finding True Love.*

Reflection:

1. Do you face any obstacles to loving yourself fully?
   a. If so, what are they?
   b. How might you overcome them?
   c. If not, how did you overcome them in the past?
2. List your strengths.
   a. Reflect on how to develop them further and share them with the world.
3. Make a list of 5 ways you will get to know yourself better in the next 3 months.
   a. Journal about each of the 5 experiences as you encounter them – what did you learn about yourself?

3

The Ethic of Integrity

Be true to yourself above all

"Conduct reveals character, and we best understand integrity when we see it lived out in a person's life."

— Charles H. Dyer

Be True To Yourself – Your True Self

It is crucial to figure out how to be true to yourself, which self to be true to, why it's important, and how to accomplish it. The traumatized self is controlled by past abuses, so that's not the self we want to be true to; otherwise we would sink deeper into those harmful patterns. The self we want to be true to is the true self, underneath all the trauma patterns. To reach the true and authentic self, we must uproot deeply buried trauma. To do this, we need help from a skilled coach (Chapter 1).

There are some signatures of the true self that help us recognize when we are reaching it. The true self demonstrates these qualities:

- ***Creative:*** producing original and innovative work, including art;
- ***Prolific:*** generating a limitless stream of ideas and content;
- ***Confident:*** grounded and secure in the true self without self-doubt or arrogance;
- ***Wonder-filled:*** displaying a genuine curiosity, desire to learn, love of and gratitude for Nature and life;
- ***Intuitive:*** able to quickly discern the real nature of any situation or person, emotionally intelligent and astute;
- ***Adaptive:*** flowing with life and its chaotic situations with suppleness.

Once we begin to live with these qualities,[6] we are living from the true self.

Do Not Please People

One of the ways we know that trauma is still controlling us is through our attitude toward others'

---

[6] There are many other qualities of the true self, and these are described in our leadership series, Book 3 (forthcoming): *The Dimensions of True Self: A Workbook for How to Live and Lead Authentically.*

expectations. If we are focused on pleasing others out of fear, to "keep the peace", or to ensure they keep liking us, we have become their slaves. To shift away from being liked to becoming authentic is the journey. It can be arduous at first, because people begin to dislike us (Chapter 2).

Instead of pleasing people and being liked, our moral compass should now point toward doing what is right and good and true. This means the course of action that demonstrates least harm, most self-love, and most integrity and compassion. Once you begin to notice that these motivate you more than being liked, you are well on your way.

Exceptions

There are exceptions to being true to you. Sometimes, violating your integrity could save a life. In the Nazi era, there were stories of people lying to save the lives of Jewish children, for example. In such cases, the ethic of avoiding harm trumps the ethic of integrity.

There are also situations where we build relationships or demonstrate love by violating our integrity. An example in my life is cooking meat for a chosen loved one. I do this to show my love for them, while violating my integrity as a vegan. My ideal dream is a plant-based kitchen where nothing ever has to die. My reality is living in our family home with loved ones; we have a shared kitchen.

My choice is to serve my loved one in ways they find comforting, which includes eating meat. When we make exceptions like these, we must be willing to live with the hypocrisy or contradiction of our actions. It is not easy, and life never is, but as we grow, we constantly learn about our limits and opportunities. Sometimes, as I have learned, I let love and harmony trump integrity.

When we examine this situation through the lens of harm, we may argue that cooking meat for our loved one harms them, because supporting them in eating meat increases their risk of lifestyle diseases. We may further contend that we are condoning harm to animals by cooking meat, which could be seen as encouraging meat-eating behavior. Both arguments are valid.

What is most interesting, however, is by choosing to love and support my loved one's harmful behavior and affirm their identity as a meat-eater, I have also created a safe space for them to reduce their meat intake to once per day or less. This means an overall reduction in harm to their health and an overall reduction in their support of harming animals.

Thus, compassion (Chapter 4) in this case has reduced overall harm, demonstrating how deeply these ethics are connected.

Now, this logic may not apply in every situation. For instance, we cannot support the murder of a few people to bring the overall number of murders down. In this case, we must end all killing. Indeed, once we extend our compassion to all life (Chapter 4), the same rule of thumb would apply to the slaughter of animals too. Each situation must be examined carefully to evaluate which ethic or ethics need to be followed for the best possible outcome in terms of harm, self-love, integrity, and compassion. This makes the ethical terrain complex, and necessary to navigate with mindfulness.

Boundaries

When it comes to integrity, we can set boundaries to support our chosen paths in life. For example, I could choose to set a boundary that I will not cook meat for anyone anymore, because I cannot condone the killing of animals. While this might create a sense of disharmony in our home, it would preserve my integrity. Boundaries come at a cost, and it's important to know which price we are willing to pay. I am not willing to alienate the family member I love and live with, so I choose to remain compromised for the sake of love.

As we navigate the dimensions of our true selves, we can choose boundaries that support and protect the limits of what is acceptable to us. If we do not do this, our integrity will be full of holes. An example of a strong boundary I have created through painful experience is to refuse to work or be in relationship with anyone who deliberately harms others. To work with willfully abusive people who refuse to change, goes against the integrity of who I am as a trauma coach and what my company stands for.

I encourage such people to change their ways, and have even coached some of them, but if they do not display the three necessary characteristics: readiness to change, willingness to do the hard work, and commitment to the self, evidenced by investment in the process,[7] I walk away. It is advisable to cut ties with anyone who refuses to acknowledge that they are abusers, and who will not work to change their harmful habits. They are not ready to stop harming people. We could love them from a distance, from within our boundaries. This is a practice of self-love and self-respect (Chapter 2).

---

[7] Based on observations of over 55 clients in our Lasting Transformation (coaching) program.

Reflection:
1. What is needed for you to live life from the true and authentic self?
    a. How do you know?
2. Which qualities of the true self listed in this chapter do you embody currently?
    a. Which do you aspire to?
    b. Why?
3. Are you a people-pleaser or do you know someone who exhibits those tendencies?
    a. How might you or they release this habit?
    b. What would it take to never go back to people-pleasing?

4

The Ethic of Compassion

Be compassionate in all your actions to all life

"Our task must be to free ourselves... by widening our circle of compassion to embrace all living creatures and the whole of nature and it's beauty."

— Albert Einstein

Cultivate Self-Compassion

As with anything, what we want to bring to the world, we must first grow and master in ourselves. Being compassionate to the self is a part of any self-love practice (Chapter 2). To treat ourselves as a best friend in practice means to actually say and do the things we would say and do for our best friend in their times of need. Some examples include showing up and listening without judgment (we can do this by journaling and using positive self-talk), encouraging ourselves, being patient, and providing a safe space to rest and recover from setbacks.

Self-compassion also makes room for us to gift ourselves with self-care practices such as meditation, yoga, journaling and reflection to clarify our points of view and manage stress and emotions. When we are kind to ourselves, our potential can radically transform, allowing us to rise above the obstacles that once held us back. Once we have mastered self-compassion, we are ready to extend our compassion to others.

Be Compassionate in your Relationships

Being compassionate and kind does not mean being "nice" or a people-pleaser (Chapter 3). In order to walk this fine line, it is important to define what compassion means to you. To have compassion means to care, have sympathy, and concern for others. To care does not mean we condone harm (Chapter 1) or neglect our self-love (Chapter 2). It means genuinely showing that you understand others and want the best for them, without compromising your integrity and boundaries (Chapter 3).

We can be compassionate with our family members, friends, and co-workers. For example, when a loved one or colleague is upset, we can listen to their perspectives and comfort them. We can let them know that we care and want to be updated about their situation. Often this is enough to help the other person feel heard and validated.

Be Humane To All Forms Of Life

As we practice compassion to the people in our lives, we strengthen our compassion muscles. We can begin to extend compassion to other forms of life: animals, plants, and the entire Earth. Being compassionate to animals, for some, may equate to not killing them or eating them. Indeed, many people are repulsed at the notion of slaughtering and eating dogs, cats, horses, and other beloved companion animals. Yet, the same feeling is not extended to cows, pigs, sheep, goats and chickens. We tend to draw the line arbitrarily somewhere when it comes to compassion for animals. The important thing is not to judge where the line is, but to actively explore why it is there.

As with my example about cooking meat while being a vegan (Chapter 3), sometimes there are interesting and deep reasons for where we draw the line. My boundary with cooking meat shows that I value my loved one, because I empathically place myself in their shoes. Food is a path to joy and togetherness, and to refuse to cook my family member's favorite foods would be hurtful. If they did the same to me, it would alienate me. Living in the same home, some compromise helps us build bridges instead of creating distance through judgment.

As we continue to learn about ourselves, and show compassion to ourselves and others, we can navigate our stance with kindness, and choosing not to place harsh judgments on our current actions. This leaves room for change in a loving way. For example, my work on plant-based wellness had led to my loved one reducing their meat intake over time as they increased their understanding of the relationships between meat and climate change, and meat and lifestyle diseases.

Indeed, love is one of the best agents of change. Self-love (Chapter 2) is the strongest foundation for dramatic change from trauma to true self. Love can also spark a change toward more compassion for all life forms. A good way to explore how you feel about animals is to read about them and get to know them. Many animals, such as pigs, chickens, cows, and dogs have social structures, emotions, personalities, and high intelligence, just like us. Even fish feel emotions. Now that's food for thought – I know, bad pun – and worth exploring.

The only way to understand compassion for all

life is to feel it, and the best way to feel it is through an awakening of the consciousness. Meditation and other contemplative practices, as well as experimentation with not eating meat are the best ways I've found to catalyze this awakening. The feeling of unhooking the self completely from cruelty is an incredible lightness of being, bringing with it tons of positive and productive energy.

Exceptions

There are situations where we cannot be compassionate. As we saw in Chapter 1, when we are being attacked physically, there might not be room for anything except a counterattack for self-defense purposes.

When we are being verbally attacked, sometimes it can be difficult to show compassion. However, with time and mindful practice, we can detach from the abuser's energy and respond in a calm and kind way, affirming our boundaries but without verbal violence. How a person treats us speaks volumes about their state of mind, and how we respond is a function of our boundaries.

Boundaries

Often, others find it easy to take advantage of compassionate people, because we tend to be caring and generous. This is certainly true for my family and me. Over time, I have learned that compassion is not the same as being a doormat. We must set boundaries with kindness but also firmness. Most importantly, the boundary must be airtight – there should not be any wiggle room for others to violate the boundary. Otherwise, they will not respect us or our boundaries.

For example, if your friend keeps borrowing money from you because they are in a financial crisis, but they don't pay it back, you need to put your foot down. You can do it with kindness and tact, but the message must be very clear. If your boundary is that you will not lend any more money until all the money owed to you is paid back, you can communicate this in a kind tone, but not budge from this line in the sand.

As you practice setting strong boundaries, your compassionate approach may help others learn to be more empowered, because you are now preventing them from taking the easy and unethical road. You are also refusing to be co-dependent with them. This nudges them to become more hard working, self-reliant and creative to cope with the challenges in their lives.

Reflection:

1. What compromises are you currently making with regard to being compassionate in relationships?
   a. Are you at peace with these compromises or not?
   b. Why?
2. How might you practice setting strong boundaries with compassion and kindness?
3. Describe a situation where you reacted without compassion.
   a. Reflect on how you might respond with kindness if that kind of situation were to recur.
4. Reflect on a time when you showed compassion to an animal.
   a. Was it an animal you would typically eat, (if you are a meat-eater)?
   b. If so, why did you show compassion in this situation?
   c. If not, why was it important to show compassion to this animal versus one you would typically consume?
5. What would it take for you to extend your compassion to all animals?

Conclusion

This book lays out four interrelated principles for how we can live more fulfilling lives. The four ethics can be summarized thus:

- *Don't intentionally harm anyone;*

- *Love yourself first so you can learn to love and be loved by others;*

- *Be true to yourself above all;*

- *Be compassionate in all your actions to all life.*

These qualities can shape our lives in meaningful ways if we practice them through our daily actions.

Achieving the four ethics requires deep self-inquiry and hard work. The key is changing our behavior. Once we are ready, willing and committed, we begin to see changes. Refer to our leadership series for more strategies:

- Published via Alchemus Prime and available via Kindle and Amazon:
    - Book 1 - *The Path to Romantic Success: What You won't Learn at School or at Home about Finding True Love*
    - Book 2 - *From Abused to Empowered: Recognizing and Releasing Behavior Patterns that come from Trauma.*
- Forthcoming:
    - Book 3 - *The Dimensions of True Self: A Workbook for How to Live and Lead Authentically*
    - Book 4 - *Career Manifestation: What it Takes to be Who You Truly Are in a World that Wants You to be Someone Else*

The road to true self, which is the foundation for a purposeful and peaceful life, is paved with behavior change. If you choose to implement the ideas in this book practically in your life starting now, it will show you the way.

At some point in the future, you will realize: it was you all along, leading the charge. It was your true self that led you to this book.

Refining ourselves so we can be authentic and

happy is a process that takes time and care. To put the guidance in this book into motion is a great first step. Keep going and see if you can live the life you were born for. This is why you are here. Everything else is a distraction.

ABOUT THE AUTHOR

Marilyn Cornelius is a behavior change specialist, coach, facilitator, author, teacher, and speaker. She supports leaders to help address climate change and wellness challenges through her multinational company, Alchemus Prime. Marilyn integrates behavioral sciences, design thinking, biomimicry and meditation techniques in novel ways using Alchemus Prime's Diamond Model. Marilyn's work implements her vision for how to live and lead in ways that are authentic, resource-efficient, adaptive to change, and beneficial to all living beings.

Marilyn has authored or co-authored 20 other popular books on self-love, trauma, and positivity; this is her 21st book. She holds a PhD in behavioral sciences and climate change from Stanford University. She has taken courses in Heartfulness, Vipassana, Mindfulness-Based Stress Reduction (MBSR), and Transcendental Meditation (TM). Marilyn has been a Reiki Master since 2009.

She has served as Chief of Staff and Coach at UN Women USA – San Francisco Bay Area Chapter, and as a Heartfulness Trainer. Her free services on social media include "Mornings with Marilyn," a daily video show; a weekly series called "Beyond Medicine"; and Dr. An, a cantankerous trauma doctor who gives an-swers.